United States Government Accountability Office

Report to Congressional Requesters

I0423783

October 2014

GROUP PURCHASING ORGANIZATIONS

Funding Structure Has Potential Implications for Medicare Costs

GAO-15-13

GAO Highlights

Highlights of GAO-15-13, a report to congressional requesters

GROUP PURCHASING ORGANIZATIONS

Funding Structure Has Potential Implications for Medicare Costs

Why GAO Did This Study

GPOs are purchasing intermediaries that negotiate contracts for medical products and services. GPOs contract with vendors and receive a fee from them when providers purchase from the vendor. These fees are a source of operating revenue for GPOs, and they are allowed to collect them if they meet the requirements of a safe harbor to the "anti-kickback" provision of the Social Security Act—known as the Anti-Kickback statute—which would otherwise prohibit such fees.

You raised questions about GPOs' contracting practices and about the impact of the GPO funding structure. This report examines (1) GPO contracting practices and the reported effects of these practices; (2) how GPOs are funded and the reported effects of this funding structure. To do this work, GAO sent a questionnaire to representatives of the 5 largest national GPOs about their contracting practices and sources of revenue; reviewed the literature on the effects of the GPO funding structure; reviewed laws, regulations, and guidance on the GPO safe harbor; interviewed representatives from HHS, FTC, the Department of Justice (DOJ), vendors, hospitals, trade associations, and economic and health care experts.

What GAO Recommends

GAO recommends that the Secretary of HHS determine whether hospitals are appropriately reporting administrative fee revenues on their Medicare cost reports and take steps to address any under-reporting that may be found. HHS agreed with the recommendation. GAO also incorporated technical comments from HHS, FTC, DOJ, and GPOs.

View GAO-15-13. For more information, contact Linda Kohn at (202) 512-7114 or kohnl@gao.gov.

What GAO Found

According to representatives from the 5 large group purchasing organizations (GPO) in GAO's review, GPO contracting generally involves three phases: (1) issue requests for proposals or invitations for vendors to competitively bid for a contract, (2) review proposals, and (3) negotiate and award contracts. GPOs reported negotiating and awarding different types of contracts to vendors in different situations. All 5 GPOs reported that the majority of the contracts they negotiate are either dual-source or multi-source, meaning that the majority of the products sold through their contracts have more than one vendor available on the GPOs' contracts. In addition, all GPOs reported that they did not bundle unrelated products and awarded mostly contracts with 3-year terms in 2012. The views of experts and others GAO interviewed on the effects of GPO contracting practices varied on issues such as whether the practices affect product innovation. In addition, while officials from the Federal Trade Commission (FTC) stated that they continue to receive and review complaints each year about GPO contracting practices, in the last 10 years, the FTC has not initiated any enforcement actions directed at GPO conduct.

The 5 GPOs in GAO's review reported being predominately funded by administrative fees collected from vendors, which were almost always based on a percentage of the purchase price of products obtained through GPO contracts. The 5 GPOs reported that these fees totaled about $2.3 billion in 2012, and nearly 70 percent of these fees were passed on to GPO customers or owners. The literature and the views of experts varied widely on the effects of this funding structure. Some suggested it creates misaligned incentives for GPOs to negotiate higher prices for medical products in order to increase the amount of vendor fees that they receive. Others suggested that competition between GPOs incentivizes them to negotiate the lowest possible prices, and mitigates these concerns. There is little empirical evidence available to either support or refute these concerns. However, to the extent that the vendor fee-based funding structure affects prices for medical products and services, Medicare payment rates may be affected over time through the annual update to hospital payment rates, which relies, in part, on information that hospitals report to the Centers for Medicare & Medicaid Services (CMS)—an agency in the Department of Health and Human Services (HHS). Moreover, Medicare payments also could be affected if hospitals do not account for revenue they receive from GPOs, which they are required to report as a reduction in costs on their cost reports. However, the extent to which hospitals are reporting this revenue is not known because this has not been reviewed by HHS since 2005, and CMS officials stated that the agency has not specifically identified this as information that should be routinely audited. Repealing the safe harbor—which allows administrative fees—could eliminate the potential effects of the GPO funding structure on Medicare payment rates, but experts and others stated that this could be disruptive to the health care supply chain at least in the near term. Over the longer term, GPOs and hospital systems are likely to adapt to the new market environment. While a repeal of the safe harbor provision would require a clearer understanding of the impact of the GPO funding structure, hospitals' potential underreporting of administrative fee revenue presents an immediate risk that can be addressed within the current GPO funding structure.

_____ United States Government Accountability Office

Contents

October 24, 2014

Congressional Requesters

Increases in health care expenditures in recent years have intensified congressional scrutiny of the costs of medical care. Federal spending for health care services provided through Medicare and Medicaid in fiscal year 2013 totaled $850.7 billion—an increase from $557.4 billion in 2006—and spending is expected to continue to increase.[1] The increase in federal spending for health care services can be attributed, in part, to the growth in health care costs, and an important component of those costs is the cost of products that hospitals and other health care providers purchase to provide care. Providers often use purchasing intermediaries known as group purchasing organizations (GPO) to negotiate contracts for products and services with vendors such as manufacturers, distributors, and other suppliers. Providers can then purchase products and services from the vendors for the prices negotiated by the GPOs.

When a provider purchases a product or service from a vendor that has a contract with a GPO, the vendor pays the GPO an administrative fee, generally based on the purchase price paid by the provider. These fees are a source of operating revenue for GPOs, and they are allowed to collect them if they meet the requirements of a safe harbor to the "anti-kickback" provision of the Social Security Act—known as the Anti-Kickback statute—which would otherwise prohibit such fees.[2] This "safe harbor" provision was enacted in 1986 to allow these payments, which

---

[1]Congressional Budget Office, *The Budget and Economic Outlook: Fiscal Years 2014 to 2024* (Washington, D.C.: Feb. 2014).

[2]The Medicare Anti-Kickback statute, enacted as a part of the Social Security Amendments of 1972, specifically prohibits the knowing or willful solicitation, receipt, offer, or payment of remuneration, including any kickback, bribe, or rebate, directly or indirectly, overtly or covertly, in cash or in kind, to induce or reward the purchase of an item or service for which payment may be made under a federal health care program. See 42 U.S.C. § 1320a-7b(b)(1)-(2).

had constituted a violation of the Anti-Kickback statute.[3] According to a House of Representatives Committee report, the Committee believed that GPOs could help reduce health care costs by enabling hospitals to obtain volume discounts from vendors and that a safe harbor should be established to ensure that GPOs and the vendors with which they contract do not risk prosecution as a result of the payment and collection of administrative fees.[4] However, the GPO funding structure protected under this safe harbor has raised questions about whether GPOs are in fact negotiating the lowest possible prices for their customers because of an inherent conflict: while GPOs represent the interests of health care providers to obtain needed products and services at a lower price, they are funded based on a percentage of the costs of products purchased from the vendors they negotiate with on behalf of providers.

Over more than a decade, members of Congress and others have raised questions about certain GPO contracting practices and the funding structure that includes vendor-paid fees. For example, questions have been raised about sole-source contracting, in which GPOs may contract with only one vendor for a given product when multiple vendors of comparable products are available; product bundling, in which price discounts are linked to purchases of a specified group of products; and long-term contracts of 5 years or more. Members of Congress have also raised questions about the oversight of GPOs by the Federal Trade Commission (FTC), the Department of Justice (DOJ), and the Department of Health and Human Services (HHS), as well as GPO self-regulation

---

[3]Omnibus Budget Reconciliation Act of 1986, Pub. L. No. 99-509, § 9321(a), 100 Stat. 1874, 2016 (Oct. 21, 1986) (codified at 42 U.S.C. § 1320a-7b(b)(3)(C)); H.R. Rep. No. 99-1012, at 309 (1986) (Conf. Rep.). In 1987, Congress directed the Department of Health and Human Services (HHS) to issue regulations designating safe harbors for various payment and business practices that would be protected from enforcement under the Anti-Kickback statute, including GPOs. See 42 C.F.R. § 1001.952(j).

[4]H.R. Rep. No. 99-727, at 72-73 (1986).

through the Healthcare Group Purchasing Industry Initiative (HGPII). We issued five reports between 2002 and 2012 related to these issues.[5]

You raised questions about GPOs' contracting practices and about the effects of the GPO funding structure.[6] This report examines

1. GPO contracting practices and the reported effects of these practices; and

2. how GPOs are funded and the reported effects of this funding structure.

To address these objectives, we sent a questionnaire to representatives of the five largest national GPOs by purchasing volume about their contracting practices and sources of revenue, including administrative fees collected from vendors.[7] We also conducted a review of the literature regarding the effects of the GPO funding structure. In addition, we reviewed documentary evidence of the factors that GPOs consider when contracting for products and services, and reviewed published articles in economic and law journals, as well as analyses of the healthcare market. We also reviewed laws, legislative history, regulations, and guidance

---

[5]See GAO, *Group Purchasing Organizations: Pilot Study Suggests Large Buying Groups Do Not Always Offer Hospitals Lower Prices*, GAO-02-690T (Washington, D.C.: April 30, 2002); *Group Purchasing Organizations: Use of Contracting Processes and Strategies to Award Contracts for Medical-Surgical Products*, GAO-03-998T (Washington, D.C.: July 16, 2003); *Group Purchasing Organizations: Research on Their Pricing Impact on Health Care Providers*, GAO-10-323R (Washington, D.C.: Jan. 29, 2010); *Group Purchasing Organizations: Services Provided to Customers and Initiatives Regarding Their Business Practices*, GAO-10-738 (Washington D.C.: Aug. 24, 2010); *Group Purchasing Organizations: Federal Oversight and Self-Regulation*, GAO-12-399R (Washington, D.C.: March 30, 2012).

[6]You also raised questions about the number of shortages of generic injectable drugs in recent years and noted that some experts had raised concerns that GPO contracting practices were a primary cause of these shortages. We issued a report and a testimony on drug shortages in February 2014 and have ongoing work focused on the causes and management of drug shortages. See GAO, *Drug Shortages: Public Health Threat Continues, Despite Efforts to Help Ensure Product Availability*, GAO-14-194 (Washington, D.C.: Feb. 10, 2014); and *Drug Shortages: Threat to Public Health Persists, Despite Actions to Help Maintain Product Availability*, GAO-14-339T (Washington, D.C.: Feb. 10, 2014).

[7]The five largest national GPOs by purchasing volume are Premier, Novation, MedAssets, HealthTrust Purchasing Group, and Amerinet. See *GPO Facts & Figures; Largest Group Purchasing Organizations* (Healthcare Purchasing News, October 2012).

related to the GPO safe harbor. We interviewed FTC, DOJ, and HHS officials about their oversight of GPOs. To obtain contextual information about their experiences with GPOs, we interviewed representatives from five hospitals and eight vendors of medical products. We selected hospitals based on variation in the number of hospital beds, the extent to which the hospital had an ownership interest in a GPO, and which GPOs they used. We selected vendors based on variation in the types of products manufactured. To determine the reported effects of the GPO funding structure, we interviewed 13 experts in economics, the healthcare market, and purchasing cooperatives. We identified these experts through our search of the relevant literature on GPOs, healthcare markets, purchasing cooperatives, and economics. We also interviewed trade associations representing GPOs and vendors of medical products. Information obtained from interviews is not generalizable. A more extensive discussion of our scope and methodology appears in appendix 1.

We conducted this performance audit from June 2013 through October 2014 in accordance with generally accepted government auditing standards. Those standards require that we plan and perform the audit to obtain sufficient, appropriate evidence to provide a reasonable basis for our findings and conclusions based on our audit objectives. We believe that the evidence obtained provides a reasonable basis for our findings and conclusions based on our audit objectives.

Background

GPOs are organizations that act as purchasing intermediaries that negotiate contracts between health care providers and vendors of medical products and services, including manufacturers, distributors, and other suppliers. The intent of GPOs is to save their customers money by pooling their purchases in order to obtain lower prices and by taking on the administrative burden of negotiating contracts with vendors. Through GPO-negotiated contracts, health care providers can purchase products from vendors, including medical devices, commodities, branded drugs, and generic drugs, as well as services, such as laundry and food services. The Healthcare Supply Chain Association (HSCA)—a trade association representing 14 healthcare GPOs—estimates that U.S. hospitals use, on average, 2 to 4 GPOs per facility, and nearly every hospital in the United States—approximately 96 percent to 98 percent—purchases through GPO contracts.

According to HSCA, the first GPO was established in 1910 by the Hospital Bureau of New York, and by the 1980s, there were more than

100 GPOs. While over 600 GPOs in various markets are currently active in the United States, a relatively small number of GPOs dominate the healthcare market for products and services sold through GPO contracts. According to HSCA, GPOs vary in size, type of ownership, and the contracting services they offer their customers. For example, some GPOs

- are owned by hospitals, while others are not.
- operate nationally, while others operate regionally to negotiate contracts with local vendors.
- serve not-for-profit hospitals, others serve for-profit hospitals, and some serve both.
- offer a broad portfolio of products and services, while others focus on specific product categories or certain types of health care, such as long-term care.

In recent years, the GPO market has become more consolidated as some large GPOs have merged. The five largest national GPOs have reported contracting for a similar, broad portfolio of products, including, for example, commodities such as cotton balls and bandages, devices such as pacemakers and stents, and branded and generic drugs. During fiscal year 2012, the 5 largest GPOs by purchasing volume reported a total purchasing volume of $130.7 billion.

Administrative Fees

During the contracting process for products and services, GPOs negotiate the payment of administrative fees by the vendor to the GPO. In addition to using these administrative fees to cover operating expenses, GPOs may distribute a portion of the fees to their health care provider customers or use them to finance other ventures, such as investing in other companies. GPOs may also use administrative fees to fund additional services outside of group purchasing for their customers, which can include custom contracting; services related to product evaluation, such as clinical evaluation and standardization of products; assessments of new technology; benchmarking data services; and marketing and insurance services.[8] (See fig. 1.)

---

[8]For additional information on services GPOs provide to their customers, see GAO-10-738.

Figure 1: General Flow of Administrative Fees

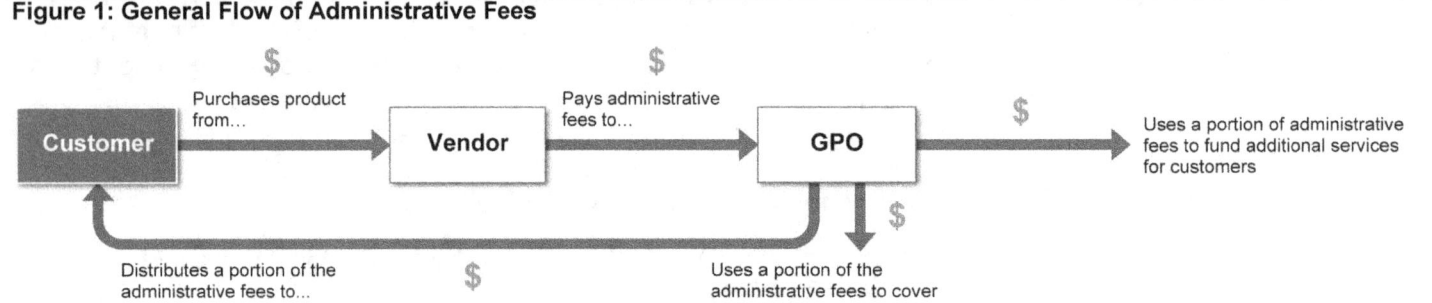

Source: GAO analysis of GPO-reported information. | GAO-15-13

Federal Oversight of GPOs

HHS

HHS's Office of the Inspector General (HHS-OIG) is responsible for enforcing the Anti-Kickback statute.[9] The Anti-Kickback statute, originally enacted in 1972 and amended over the years, generally prohibits the knowing or willful receipt or payment of fees to induce or reward the purchase of an item or service for which payment may be made under a federal health care program.[10] According to HHS-OIG, the main purpose of the Anti-Kickback statute is to protect patients and federal health care programs, including Medicare, from fraud and abuse by curtailing the corrupting influence of money on health care decisions.[11] In 1986 Congress added a "safe harbor" provision to the Anti-Kickback statute to allow for fees paid by vendors to a GPO.[12] In addition, in 1991, HHS-OIG issued a regulation establishing the requirements that GPOs must meet in

---

[9]HHS-OIG shares this responsibility with DOJ.

[10]The statute specifically prohibits the knowing or willful solicitation, receipt, offer, or payment of remuneration, including any kickback, bribe, or rebate, directly or indirectly, overtly or covertly, in cash or in kind, to induce or reward the purchase of an item or service for which payment may be made under a federal health care program.

[11]Department of Health and Human Services Office of Inspector General, *Fact Sheet: Federal Anti-Kickback Law and Regulatory Safe Harbors*, (Washington, D.C.: November 1999).

[12]Omnibus Budget Reconciliation Act of 1986, Pub. L. No. 99-509, § 9321(a), 100 Stat. 1874, 2016 (codified at 42 U.S.C. § 1320a-7b(b)(3)(C)).

order to qualify for safe harbor protection under the Anti-Kickback statute.[13] Under the regulation, a GPO must

- have a written agreement with its customers either stating that the contract administrative fees are to be 3 percent or less of the purchase price, or specifying the amount or maximum amount that each vendor will pay; and

- disclose in writing to each customer, at least annually, and to the Secretary of HHS upon request, the amount of contract administrative fees received from each vendor with respect to purchases made by or on behalf of the customer.[14]

The GPO safe harbor statutory provision and regulation do not require HHS-OIG to routinely review or monitor GPO written agreements and disclosures. However, HHS-OIG has the authority to investigate potential violations of the Anti-Kickback statute. HHS-OIG also has the authority to impose administrative penalties, including civil money penalties, and exclusion from federal health care programs on GPOs that violate the statute.[15] HHS-OIG also may refer such violations to DOJ, which in turn may bring criminal and civil actions against GPOs that it determines to have violated the Anti-Kickback statute.[16] HHS-OIG does not have

---

[13]See 42 C.F.R. § 1001.952(j). In 1987, Congress directed HHS to issue regulations designating safe harbors for various payment and business practices that would be protected from enforcement under the Anti-Kickback statute, including GPOs. Medicare and Medicaid Patient and Program Protection Act of 1987, Pub. L. No. 100-93, § 14, 101 Stat. 680, 697. HHS-OIG refers to the statutory provision as an "exception" and the regulation as a "safe harbor." In this report, we refer to each as a "safe harbor."

[14]To qualify for safe harbor protection, a GPO must be authorized to act as a purchasing agent for a group of individuals or entities that provide services for which payment may be made under a federal health care program and who are neither wholly owned by the GPO nor subsidiaries of a parent corporation that wholly owns the GPO, either directly or through another wholly-owned entity. See 42 C.F.R. § 1001.952(j). GPOs that are uncertain as to whether their arrangements qualify for safe harbor protection may request an advisory opinion from HHS-OIG. 42 U.S.C. § 1320a-7d(b).

[15]See 42 U.S.C. §§ 1320a-7(b)(7), 1320a-7a(a)(7).

[16]DOJ may bring civil actions against GPOs that violate the Anti-Kickback statute under the False Claims Act. The False Claims Act is a federal fraud and abuse law that prohibits knowingly presenting, or causing to be presented, a false or fraudulent claim for federal payment. 31 U.S.C. §§ 3729-3733. A Medicare claim that results from a kickback may render it false or fraudulent, creating liability under the civil False Claims Act as well as the Anti-Kickback statute. See 31 U.S.C. §§ 3729-3733.

general oversight authority over GPOs because GPOs do not directly participate in Medicare and, therefore, do not enter provider agreements with the Centers for Medicare & Medicaid Services (CMS)—a component of HHS.

In 2012, we found that, according to officials from HHS-OIG, the office had not routinely exercised its authority to request and review disclosures related to GPOs' administrative fees, but it had collected information on GPOs' administrative fees while conducting audits of hospitals' cost reports.[17] The provision and receipt of discounts, rebates, and net revenue distributions by GPOs to hospitals is protected from prosecution under the Anti-Kickback statute by another provision—known as the "discount safe harbor." Specifically, a discount or other reduction in price obtained by a Medicare or Medicaid provider is protected from prosecution if the reduction in price is properly disclosed and appropriately reflected in the provider's Medicare, or applicable state Medicaid, cost report.[18]

HHS-OIG conducted two audits in 2005 in which it reviewed the administrative fees that six national GPOs received from vendors and how selected customers of the GPOs accounted for revenue distributions from the GPOs on their Medicare cost reports.[19] The cost reports are used, in part, to set hospital payment rates for Medicare. HHS-OIG found that some of the GPO customers did not fully account for revenue

---

[17] See GAO-12-399R. Medicare certified institutional providers, such as hospitals, are required to submit an annual cost report to a fiscal intermediary, a Medicare contractor. The cost report contains provider information such as facility characteristics, utilization data, costs and charges by cost center, Medicare settlement data, and financial statement data. Medicare contractors use these data to compute some elements of Medicare reimbursement. The information in cost reports is one of the primary sources that the Medicare Payment Advisory Commission uses in reviewing the reasonableness of Medicare payment levels.

[18] 42 U.S.C. § 1320a-7b(b)(3)(A); 42 C.F.R. 1001.952(h). Medicare regulations also generally require health care providers to offset purchase discounts, allowances, and refunds of expenses against expenses on their Medicare cost reports. 42 C.F.R. § 413.98.

[19] See Department of Health and Human Services, Office of Inspector General, *Review of Revenue From Vendors at Three Group Purchasing Organizations and Their Members*, A-05-03-00074 (Washington, D.C.: January 2005) and *Review of Revenue From Vendors at Three Additional Group Purchasing Organizations and Their Members*, A-05-04-00073 (Washington, D.C.: May 2005).

GAO-15-13 Group Purchasing Organizations

distributions from the GPOs on their Medicare cost reports.[20] HHS-OIG recommended that CMS provide specific guidance on the proper treatment of revenue distributions received from GPOs on Medicare cost reports. In December 2011, CMS issued an update to its provider manual specifying that these distributions must be properly accounted for on the cost reports.

DOJ and FTC

DOJ and FTC are responsible for enforcing federal antitrust laws, which GPOs are required to follow.[21] The agencies have the authority to investigate a GPO's potential violation of federal antitrust laws, identified either through a complaint filed with the agencies, through notification of a merger, or through information obtained through the agencies' own efforts. The agencies have the authority to resolve violations in a number of ways ranging from compliance under a consent order, to an administrative complaint, to filing a criminal or civil suit.[22] In addition to its antitrust enforcement authority, DOJ also has the authority to bring criminal and civil actions against GPOs that it determines to have violated the Anti-Kickback statute.

---

[20]For example, in its January 2005 report, HHS-OIG reviewed how 21 hospitals accounted for the net revenue distributed by 3 GPOs. They found that these hospitals did not fully account for the net revenue distributions on their Medicare cost reports. Specifically, while members of one GPO offset 92 percent of distributions, members of another offset only 54 percent. In total, the 21 members offset 78 percent of revenue distributed by GPOs. In addition, in a May 2005 report, HHS-OIG reviewed Medicare cost reports for 38 hospitals under 7 health care systems that received a total of $123 million in administrative fee revenue. They found that one of the health care systems did not fully account for net revenue distributions on its Medicare cost reports. As a result, administrative fees of about $5 million related to 6 of the 38 hospitals reviewed were not offset on Medicare cost reports.

[21]The Sherman Act is enforced by DOJ and prohibits restraints of trade and monopolization. See 15 U.S.C. §§ 1-7. The Federal Trade Commission Act, enforced by FTC, bans unfair methods of competition and unfair or deceptive acts or practices. See 15 U.S.C. §§ 41-58. The Clayton Act, jointly enforced by DOJ and FTC, regulates mergers and acquisitions, among other things, and gives DOJ and FTC, under the Hart-Scott-Rodino Amendments to the Clayton Act, the authority to review certain proposed mergers before they occur. See 15 U.S.C. §§ 12-27.

[22]A consent order is a voluntary settlement agreement entered into by FTC and an individual or entity that the agency has alleged is engaged in activity that violates the Federal Trade Commission Act or the Clayton Act. See 16 C.F.R. §§ 2.31-2.34. Voluntary settlement agreements entered into by DOJ, often known as consent decrees, are filed in federal district court to resolve a legal challenge by DOJ and are approved by the court upon a finding that they are in the public interest. 15 U.S.C. § 16 (b)-(h).

In 2012, we found that DOJ and FTC had investigated complaints against GPOs. We identified one lawsuit filed by DOJ against a GPO, while FTC officials told us the agency had not taken any enforcement action against a GPO since 2004.[23] Officials said that while FTC has investigated GPOs to determine whether their behavior was anticompetitive, the agency has not brought any cases to court or issued any consent orders. An FTC official told us that in order to take enforcement action against a GPO, FTC would need to determine that a GPO violated the law and an enforcement action was in the public interest.

GPOs Reported Generally Utilizing a Three-Phased Approach to Competitively Negotiate Contracts with Vendors

According to the GPOs in our review, GPO contracting generally involves three phases: (1) issue requests for proposals (RFP) or invitations for vendors to competitively bid for a contract, (2) review proposals, and (3) negotiate and award contracts. (See fig. 2.)

Figure 2: GPOs' Three-Phased Competitive Bidding Approach to Negotiating Contracts

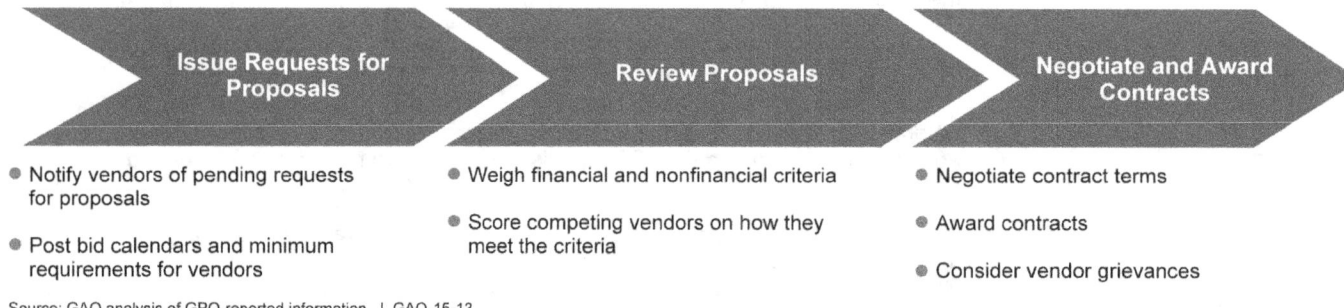

Issue Requests for Proposals
- Notify vendors of pending requests for proposals
- Post bid calendars and minimum requirements for vendors

Review Proposals
- Weigh financial and nonfinancial criteria
- Score competing vendors on how they meet the criteria

Negotiate and Award Contracts
- Negotiate contract terms
- Award contracts
- Consider vendor grievances

Source: GAO analysis of GPO-reported information. | GAO-15-13

---

[23]In 2007, DOJ challenged actions by a GPO for temporary nursing services and its member hospitals, alleging that the GPO caused the wages paid to temporary nurses in Arizona to fall below competitive levels. See *U.S. v. Ariz. Hosp. and Healthcare Assn.*, CV07-1030-PHX (D.Ariz. filed May 22, 2007).

Issue RFPs. Representatives from all five GPOs in our review reported generally issuing RFPs as part of an open bidding process for products and services to place on contract. Issuing RFPs includes notifying vendors, and publicly posting information such as bid calendars, minimum requirements for vendors, and criteria that the GPOs will weigh when considering competing proposals. All five GPOs in our review have posted on their websites information about the minimum requirements that vendors must meet. For example, one GPO's website states that vendors must be the original equipment manufacturer or demonstrate an exclusive marketing relationship for the products included in the RFP, among other things. Another GPO specifies meeting minimum levels of product quality, durability, and cost-effectiveness, as well as requirements for the financial stability and long-term viability of the vendor. A sample RFP provided by a GPO states that during the competitive bidding process, it will consider a vendor's product capabilities, maintenance, and ability to upgrade, as well as pricing and other financial factors.

Four of the five GPOs in our review reported that under certain limited circumstances, they may award contracts to vendors without issuing RFPs. For example, these "non-bid" contracts may be awarded to vendors that present a proprietary, patented, or innovative product; if a small group of customers request a local or regional vendor contract; or if a product supply shortage or other unique circumstances arise. The fifth GPO reported that all contracts are awarded through a competitive bidding process, even if there is only one bidder. A representative from one generic drug manufacturer stated that, while there is not much opportunity for innovation in the generic drug market, GPOs will award contracts outside of the three-phased competitive bidding process to vendors that have innovative packaging—such as flip-top vials versus a pre-mixed bag—if it benefits their customers. A representative from this manufacturer stated that GPO contracts with vendors generally contain provisions that the GPOs have the right to add additional vendors of the same product if the other vendor has innovative packaging.

Review proposals. All five GPOs in our review reported considering multiple aspects of a vendor and product when reviewing proposals, including weighing financial and nonfinancial criteria, and then scoring competing vendors in order to inform their contracting decisions.[24] For example, one GPO reported reviewing aspects such as a vendor's ability to provide sufficient product to its customers, any documentation of concerns raised by Food and Drug Administration (FDA) inspections, quality and safety of the products, the source of raw materials, and bar code readability. A representative from another GPO said that the GPO considers the "total value" of a product or service for their customers, not necessarily solely the price. The total value includes, for example, product quality, upfront price, discounts, rebates, and anticipated administrative fee revenue. This representative said that in certain situations, such as with multiple possible suppliers of a product, a GPO customer would not necessarily want to purchase the product with the lowest price.

Negotiate and award contracts. GPOs reported negotiating and awarding different types of contracts to vendors in different situations. All five of the GPOs in our review reported that the majority of the contracts they negotiate are either dual-source or multi-source, meaning that the majority of the products sold through their contracts have more than one vendor available on the GPOs' contracts. In addition, all five GPOs reported that they did not bundle unrelated products, and awarded mostly contracts with 3-year terms in 2012. All five GPOs also reported including provisions in some contracts—referred to as commitment provisions—in which customers that purchase a certain percent of product volume receive a rebate or reduced price. For example, a vendor might offer greater discounts to GPO customers that purchase at least 80 percent of a certain group of products from that manufacturer. Commitment requirements can also be tiered, resulting in the opportunity for a customer to commit to different percentages of purchasing volume: the higher the percentage, the lower the price.

Representatives from all five GPOs also reported that, in certain situations, they negotiated sole-source contracts, contracts that bundled related products, and long-term contracts of 5 years or more. All five

---

[24]GPOs have reported being advised by committees consisting of clinical, pharmacy, and technical experts from their customers—such as physicians and nurses who would be using the products and services being evaluated—in making contracting decisions. According to the GPOs, these committees consider customer needs, product quality, and pricing before making recommendations for to the GPOs about products and services to place on GPO contracts.

GPOs in our review reported that their contracting practices have not changed much over time.

- *Sole-source contracts*: All five GPOs reported that they do negotiate sole-source contracts when it is advantageous to their customers, though some GPOs reported negotiating a higher proportion of sole-source contracts than others. One GPO said that about 18 percent of its customers' spending through the GPO is through sole-source contracts. Three GPOs reported sole-source contracting for branded drugs and commodities, and four GPOs reported sole-source contracting for generic drugs, including generic injectable drugs. For example, one GPO reported that in 2012 it had sole-source contracts in effect for generic drugs including an oncology drug—oxaliplatin, and an antiviral—acyclovir. Representatives from this GPO reported taking a vendor's performance and supply capacity into consideration when determining whether to sole-source contract with a vendor. For example, the representatives stated that the GPO no longer sole-source contracts with a vendor that had failed to comply with FDA standards. Representatives from one vendor stated that, as a result of recent drug shortages, some GPOs have developed a philosophy to contract with as many vendors as possible to ensure a continuous supply for their customers, but that other GPOs choose to contract with a limited number of vendors and hold those vendors accountable for supplying their customers.

- *Contracts that bundle related products*: Representatives from all five GPOs in our review reported negotiating contracts that offer discounts based on the purchase of bundled products, but restricting bundling to products that are used together or are otherwise related in order to create efficiencies and help standardize products for their customers. Several GPOs reported bundling related commodities, and one GPO reported bundling related branded pharmaceuticals. Representatives from one GPO stated that the GPO bundles related products in the same product category, such as intravenous (IV) sets and solutions, diapers and underpads for incontinence care, and mobility aids such as walkers, crutches, and canes. Representatives from another GPO stated, for example, that it negotiates bundled contracts for interventional coronary products including stents, balloons, catheters, and guide wires. In addition, another GPO reported that, in 2013, it implemented a program through which participating customers can standardize their purchases for up to 40 commodity categories for additional discounts.

- *Long-term contracts*: Representatives from all five GPOs reported awarding longer terms for certain types of products, such as IV systems and laboratory products. One GPO reported that its customers requested long-term contracts for IV systems because they found it difficult to switch IVs and pumps every 3 years, and one manufacturer we interviewed stated that the investment in time and money needed to train clinicians in how to use a brand of IV products makes it inconvenient and disruptive for hospitals to change these products. A representative from another GPO stated that they often negotiate longer-term contracts for chemistry analyzers and the specific reagents that are used with them, and had recently negotiated a 7-year contract for both the analyzers and reagents together.

Finally, all 5 GPOs in our review provide a grievance process for vendors who are not awarded contracts. A representative of one GPO stated that, when vendors are not awarded a contract and want to know why, GPO staff debrief the vendor on how to make changes to increase their chances of being awarded a contract during the next RFP cycle. After this debrief, a representative of the GPO stated that vendors can file a formal grievance with the GPO. Another GPO posted on its website that any vendor may file a grievance within 30 days of the announcement of the contract award. The website states that the GPO will acknowledge receipt of the grievance immediately, and provide a detailed response within 90 days, including the GPO's rationale for the final decision. In addition to each GPO's separate grievance processes, HGPII—which GPOs formed in 2005 in order to promote best practices and public accountability among member GPOs—also has a formal grievance process that vendors may use to lodge complaints against GPOs. However, HGPII representatives told us that no complaints have been formally submitted. They explained that, while it is possible that there are no vendor complaints, they believe it is more likely that not enough vendors know about the grievance process. HGPII representatives stated that they have brought on board an in-house ethicist to review HGPII's grievance process.

The views of experts and others we interviewed on the effects of GPO contracting practices varied. For example, some experts and other stakeholders contend that GPOs' contracting practices may result in a reduction in product innovation. Specifically, one expert said that if manufacturers believe that it is impossible to get onto a GPO contract, but that such a contract is necessary for market success, then manufacturers will not innovate and create new products. However, others we interviewed told us that GPO contracting practices do not block access to innovative products. For example, all 5 of the largest GPOs reported using a competitive bidding process as well as contract clauses that allow for innovative products to be placed on existing contracts. The GPOs in our review also reported participating in forums to help identify new, potentially innovative, products in the marketplace. However, they said vendors of products that are essentially the same as other products already on GPO contracts need to compete through the competitive bidding process for the opportunity to be awarded a contract. While officials from the FTC told us that they continue to receive complaints each year about the potential anticompetitive effects of GPO contracting practices—including complaints that GPOs have contributed to recent shortages of generic injectable drugs—in the last ten years, the FTC has not initiated any enforcement actions directed at GPO conduct. FTC staff explained that they have faced significant challenges in investigating allegations of anticompetitive behavior of GPOs due to a lack of data. They stated that there are a number of significant methodological challenges related to conducting a rigorous economic analysis of the GPO industry. In addition, a DOJ official told us that the agency has not brought any actions or issued any guidance on GPOs since 2007.[25] He also stated that the DOJ has received one GPO-related complaint since 2012 when our most recent prior report was issued.

---

[25]In 2007, DOJ challenged actions by a GPO for temporary nursing services and its member hospitals, alleging that the GPO caused the wages paid to temporary nurses in Arizona to fall below competitive levels. In May, 2007, DOJ reached a settlement with the GPO, which prohibits the GPO and its hospital customers from agreeing on competitively sensitive contract terms between hospitals and nursing staff agencies, including uniform bill rates paid to nursing staff agencies. The consent decree also prohibits the GPO from circumventing the settlement by engaging in anticompetitive activity, such as boycotts or other discriminatory conduct, against nonparticipating nursing agencies or any hospitals that sought to use them. The GPO that was the subject of this lawsuit was not one of the GPOs included in our review. See *U.S. v. Ariz. Hosp. and Healthcare Assn.*, CV07-1030-PHX (D.Ariz. filed May 22, 2007).

While Experts' Views on the Effects of Vendor Funding of GPOs Varied, the Funding Structure May Affect Medicare Payment

The five GPOs in our review reported being predominately funded by administrative fees collected from vendors, and the experts' views of the effects of this funding structure varied widely. In addition, the GPO funding structure may affect Medicare payments over time.

GPOs Reported Being Predominately Funded by Vendors

The five GPOs in our review reported being predominately funded by administrative fees collected from vendors, which were almost always based on a percentage of the purchase price for products obtained through GPO contracts. GPOs use these fees to fund their operating expenses, including expenses related to contracting with vendors and providing additional services to their customers outside of group purchasing.[26] On average, the five GPOs in our review reported that administrative fees collected from vendors accounted for about 92 percent of their revenue in 2012, ranging from a low of 83 percent to a high of 98 percent.[27] In addition, these GPOs reported receiving, on average, 3.3 percent of their revenue from member fees, ranging from 0.2 percent to 12.1 percent. Member fees included, for example, fees that a GPO charged hospitals in exchange for membership in the GPO. The five GPOs also reported that revenue from outside investments accounted for, on average, 2.2 percent of their revenue in 2012. However, only two GPOs reported receiving this type of revenue, which accounted for 8.1 percent and 2.7 percent of their total revenue in 2012, respectively. This revenue included, for example, equity income from an ownership interest in another GPO. Finally, the GPOs reported receiving, on average, 0.6 percent of their revenue from other sources, ranging from 0 percent to 1.5 percent. This other revenue included, for example,

---

[26]Four of the five GPOs in our review reported using administrative fees to fund additional services outside of group purchasing for their customers in 2012. Services funded with administrative fees included, for example, benchmarking data, equipment repair, patient safety services, and marketing of products and services. Representatives from GPOs we interviewed stated that their hospital customers are increasingly requesting these additional services.

[27]GPOs reported data by fiscal year, and these fiscal years varied.

vendor exhibit fees and conference fees. In addition to these sources of revenue, two of the five GPOs in our review offered private label programs to their hospital customers in 2012. Under these programs, vendors may pay the GPOs licensing fees—which are also based on a percentage of the purchase price of products—to market their products using the GPO's brand name. On average, the 5 GPOs reported that licensing fees accounted for 2.2 percent of their revenue, though only two of the GPOs in our review collected licensing fees through private labeling programs in 2012. (See fig. 3)

Figure 3: Average Percentage Distribution of the Reported Sources of Revenue in 2012 for the Five Largest National GPOs

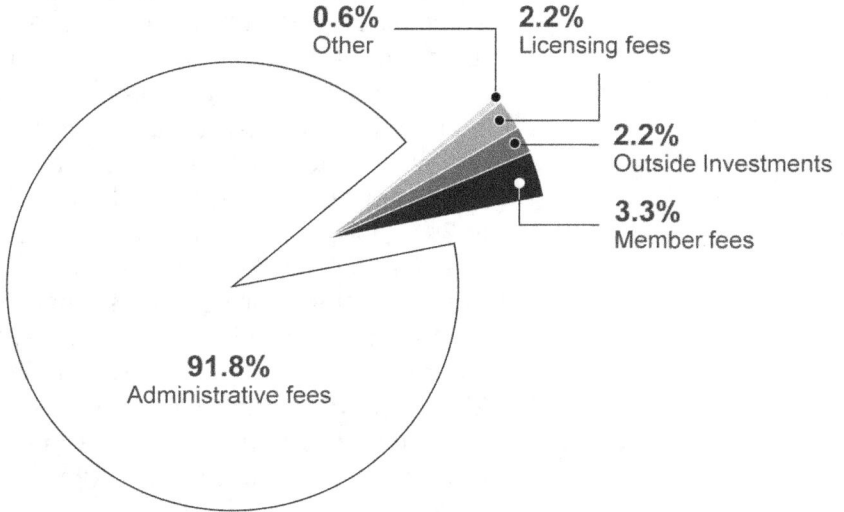

Source: GAO analysis of GPO-reported information. | GAO-15-13

Note: These percentages reflect the average of the percentages reported by each GPO in fiscal year 2012, and GPOs' fiscal years varied. Only two of the five largest GPOs collected licensing fees in fiscal year 2012.

The GPOs in our review generally reported receiving more fees from vendors in 2012 than they did in 2008. Together, all five GPOs reported collecting a total of $2.3 billion in administrative and licensing fees from vendors in 2012.[28] This represents a 20 percent increase in the total amount of fees collected from vendors in 2008, when adjusted for

---

[28]Throughout this report, we also refer to fees collected from vendors, such as administrative and licensing fees, as "vendor fees."

inflation. One GPO reported no change in the total amount of vendor fees collected between 2008 and 2012, but did report a 15 percent increase in its percentage of revenue from outside investments. The other four GPOs reported increases in the total amount of vendor fees collected between 2008 and 2012, ranging from 13 percent to 53 percent, when adjusted for inflation. GPO representatives told us there were many reasons for the growth in volume of fees collected, including increases in purchasing volume by customers and additional products being added to contracts. Although we requested this information for years prior to 2008, two of the five GPOs in our review reported that they were unable to provide it because they do not retain records for that long.

All five GPOs in our review reported most frequently receiving administrative fees from vendors that were at or below 3 percent,[29] although the two GPOs with private-label programs reported also receiving licensing fees from vendors of products sold under the GPOs' brand names in addition to administrative fees. All five GPOs in our review reported that the most frequent vendor fee they received in 2012 was 3 percent. In addition, all five GPOs reported average fees received in 2012, weighted by purchasing volume, of around 1 to 2 percent. This average includes fees from distributors and manufacturers. Because fees from distributors are often less than 1 percent, average fees from manufacturers are likely to be higher than the 1 to 2 percent overall average. In addition, the three GPOs without private-label programs in 2012 reported that the highest vendor fee they received that year was 3 percent. The administrative fee percentages that GPOs reported receiving in 2012 are consistent with the levels that the GPOs reported for 2008.

The two GPOs with private-label programs in 2012 reported that their highest fees—9.9 and 11.12 percent—were for products sold through their private-label programs and included both an administrative fee as well as a licensing fee for the GPO to market the products to their customers. Representatives from the GPO that reported the fee of 9.9 percent stated that this was for a brand name drug with a variable fee based on the vendor's sales volume—the vendor was willing to pay a higher fee in exchange for the GPO's customers pre-ordering the drug.

---

[29]The GPO safe harbor regulation requires that agreements between GPOs and their customers specify either that the contract administrative fees are to be 3 percent or less of the purchase price, or specify the amount or maximum amount that each vendor will pay.

GAO-15-13 Group Purchasing Organizations

Representatives from the GPO that reported the 11.12 percent fee stated that the fee was negotiated with a vendor that supplied five generic drugs through the GPO's private-label program.

Average fee percentages, weighted by purchasing volume, that GPOs reported receiving in 2012 were generally consistent across different categories of products, but there were some small differences. For example, fees for branded drugs were generally lower than for generic drugs—average fees for branded drugs ranged from 0.86 percent to 2.08 percent, while average fees for generic drugs ranged from 1.31 percent to 3.62 percent. Four of the 5 GPOs reported that, of the total amount of vendor fees they received in 2012, on average, 25 percent were for commodities, 15 percent were for devices, 12 percent were for brand name drugs, and 8 percent were for generic drugs. The remaining 41 percent were for other products and services, such as capital equipment and food service. The fifth GPO in our review was unable to report information separately for devices and commodities.

Experts' Views on the Effects of the GPO Funding Structure Varied Widely, Though Empirical Data on the Effects Are Limited

The literature we reviewed and the views of experts we interviewed varied widely on the effects of the GPO funding structure, specifically the reliance on vendor fees. Some of the literature we reviewed and experts we interviewed asserted that the vendor fee-based funding structure of GPOs creates misaligned incentives for them to negotiate higher prices for medical products in order to increase the amount of vendor fees that that they receive. Several experts that we interviewed stated that, based on economic theory, the GPO funding structure creates a principal-agent problem, in which the GPOs are motivated to act in their own best interests, rather than the best interests of their customers. These experts argued that because the GPOs' compensation increases as prices increase, the GPOs have little incentive to negotiate lower prices, even though their customers would benefit from lower prices. Therefore, GPOs may place greater weight on the administrative and other fees than the prices of products and services for their customers. According to these experts, this funding structure—which allows vendors to pay administrative fees to GPOs—distorts the bidding process and results in inflated prices for hospitals relative to a funding structure where these administrative fees are not allowed.

Other people we interviewed—including some experts and representatives of the GPOs—stated that competition between GPOs to retain their customers incentivizes them to negotiate the lowest possible prices, and mitigates any theoretical principal-agent problem. They explained that hospitals can switch GPOs anytime if they are not satisfied with the prices that a GPO is negotiating. Representatives from one hospital said that hospitals switch GPOs when they merge with larger systems, but that there are significant costs related to the conversion. Several experts reported that not only are the largest national GPOs in intense competition with each other, they are in competition for purchases made directly from manufacturers, as well as through regional GPOs, and hospital and health system alliances. Specifically, one expert we interviewed stated that GPO customers often obtain pricing information from all possible sources and then selectively choose products and services they can obtain for the best prices. Another expert told us that the percentage-based administrative fee structure works well because GPOs are only compensated for the sales that are made.

Although some experts have reported potential effects of the GPO funding structure, empirical data on the effects are limited. We identified one study that presented empirical data on the effects of the vendor-fee-based GPO funding structure.[30] The authors of this study concluded that, if the GPO safe harbor provision were eliminated, then GPOs "would likely structure their procurement process in a way that elicited more competitive bidding, resulting in lower prices and greater competition." In addition, the authors concluded that altering the GPO funding structure would not eliminate any efficiencies that GPOs currently offer, such as reduced transaction costs or consolidated buying power. We also found other studies that presented empirical data focused more broadly on the value of GPOs, such as studies that focused on whether GPOs save their customers money.[31] However, these studies did not include empirical evidence that directly addressed the effects of the GPO funding structure.

---

[30]R.E. Litan, H.J. Singer, and A. Birkenbach, "An Empirical Analysis of Aftermarket Transactions by Hospitals," *The Journal of Contemporary Health Law and Policy*, vol. XXVIII: 1 (2011). The authors of this study told us that the data were purchased through a grant received by the Medical Device Manufacturers Association. For a rebuttal of this study, see C.A. Johnston and C.D. Rooney, "GPOs and the Healthcare Supply Chain: Market-Based Solutions and Real-World Recommendations to Reduce Pricing Secrecy and Benefit Healthcare Providers," *The Journal of Contemporary Health Law and Policy*, vol. XXIX: 1 (2012).

[31]See, for example, E.S. Schneller, "The Value of Group Purchasing – 2009: Meeting the Needs for Strategic Savings" (2009); D.E. Goldenberg & R. King, "A 2008 Update of Cost Savings and a Marketplace Analysis of the Health Care Group Purchasing Industry" (2009).

The GPO Funding Structure May Affect Medicare Payments over Time

The GPO funding structure may affect Medicare payments over time.[32] To the extent that the vendor-fee-based funding structure affects prices for medical products and services—either by reducing or inflating the costs of the products and services—Medicare payment rates may be affected over time through the annual update to the Prospective Payment System hospital payment rates. According to HHS, these updates rely, in part, on information reported by hospitals on their Medicare cost reports, which reflect the hospitals' costs of medical supplies, including those purchased through GPOs.[33]

Moreover, Medicare payments could be affected if hospitals do not appropriately account for any revenues they receive from GPOs. These revenues are required to be reported as a reduction in costs on hospitals' costs reports. All five GPOs in our review reported passing a percentage of the administrative fees—in some cases, the majority of fees collected from vendors—on to their customers or owners in 2012. All five GPOs reported sharing with their customers or owners between 37.6 percent and 100 percent of the total administrative fees they received in 2012—a total of $1.6 billion.[34] This represents 70 percent of the $2.3 billion in administrative fees collected in 2012. The amount distributed to customers and owners ranged from $54 million to $472 million per GPO. To the extent that administrative fee revenue is not reflected on cost reports, Medicare could be overpaying hospitals. The extent to which

---

[32]For additional information on this topic, see GAO-12-399R.

[33]In addition, the Medicare Payment Advisory Commission (MedPAC) uses the cost reports as one component in their assessment of the adequacy of payment rates. MedPAC is an independent congressional agency established by the Balanced Budget Act of 1997 to advise the U.S. Congress on issues affecting the Medicare program. Annually, MedPAC assesses the adequacy of Medicare payments and recommends to Congress whether base payment rates should be changed. MedPAC's general approach is to ensure enough funding is available to ensure payments are adequate to cover the costs of an efficient provider and to improve payment accuracy among services and providers. Among several factors considered in this assessment are Medicare payment and provider costs for the current year using information reported by hospitals to CMS on their cost reports in order to examine the relationship between payments and costs. The annual assessment of payment adequacy also considers whether payments should be updated for the coming year based on anticipated changes in costs.

[34]One GPO reported returning 100 percent of administrative fees to its legacy owners, who then fund the GPOs' operating expenses. This GPO reported that its legacy owners include the original partners who started the company, including their successors. In addition to the legacy owners, the GPO reported distributing administrative fee revenue to customers of the GPO who have a "fee-sharing agreement" with the GPO.

hospitals are reporting this additional revenue is not known because HHS-OIG has not reviewed cost reports for this information since 2005.[35] In addition, CMS officials told us that the agency has not specifically identified this as information that should be routinely audited by Medicare Audit Contractors.

Some experts that we interviewed stated that the potential effects of the GPO funding structure on Medicare payment rates could be eliminated if the GPO safe harbor were repealed and GPOs were no longer permitted to collect fees from vendors. However, experts and representatives from vendors, GPOs, and hospitals we interviewed stated that there would be a disruption to hospitals and vendors while they transitioned to a new supply chain model. Others we interviewed—including GPO representatives—told us that if the safe harbor were repealed, GPOs would eventually cease to exist because hospitals would not be able to afford to pay the fees. However, some hospitals already pay directly for access to contracts to supplement their existing contracting arrangements with their GPOs. For example, a wholly-owned subsidiary of one large, national GPO charges its customers a $50,000 a year subscription fee for access to a web-based system for viewing hospital supply prices, negotiating contracts with vendors directly, and tracking their purchases and contracts online. The company has reported more than $10 billion in purchasing power from a user base of 600 hospitals in its first year. Finally, others stated that, if the safe harbor were repealed, smaller hospitals might have more difficulty adjusting and may be more likely to merge with larger hospital systems.

Conclusions

Congress passed the GPO safe harbor provision because it believed that GPOs could help reduce health care costs by enabling hospitals to obtain volume discounts from vendors. However, the GPO funding structure protected under the safe harbor—specifically, the payment of administrative fees by vendors based on a percentage of the cost of the

---

[35]In a January 2005 report, HHS-OIG reported that none of the 21 GPO customers it reviewed fully accounted for revenue distributions they received from the GPOs on their Medicare cost reports—while customers of one GPO offset 92 percent of distributions, customers of another GPO offset only 54 percent. HHS-OIG reported that, in total, the 21 customers offset on their Medicare cost reports $200 million of the $255 million distributed by the GPOs. See Department of Health and Human Services, Office of Inspector General, Review of Revenue From Vendors at Three Group Purchasing Organizations and Their Members, A-05-03-00074 (Washington, D.C.: January 2005).

products or services—raises questions about whether GPOs are actually negotiating the lowest prices. Some experts believe there is an incentive for GPOs to negotiate higher prices for products and services because GPO compensation increases as prices increase. However, other experts, as well as GPOs, stated that there is sufficient competition between them to mitigate any potential conflicts of interest. Almost 30 years after its passage, there is little empirical evidence to definitively assess the impact of the vendor-fee-based funding structure protected under the safe harbor. While repealing the safe harbor could eliminate misaligned incentives, most agree there would be a disruption while hospitals and vendors transitioned to new arrangements. Over the longer term, if the current trend of hospital consolidation continues, the concerns about these disruptions may be diminished to the extent that large hospital systems may be in a better position to pay GPOs directly for their services or negotiate contracts with vendors on their own. Furthermore, given that some hospitals are already paying a subsidiary of one GPO directly for access to vendor contracts, alternative approaches are possible.

Despite the limited evidence on the impact of the vendor-fee-based funding structure protected under the safe harbor, there is a potential impact on the Medicare program. To the extent that the funding structure has the potential to affect the costs of products and services, periodic updates of Medicare's payment rates will incorporate these costs over time. Additionally, GPOs distribute to their owners and customers— mostly hospitals—a percentage of the administrative fees they collect from vendors, in some cases the majority of such fees. Hospitals are required by federal law to account for this revenue in reports to Medicare, but that has not always occurred. In 2005, HHS-OIG found that some GPO customers did not fully account for GPO revenue distributions on their Medicare cost reports. Subsequently, CMS issued updated guidance specifying that these distributions must be properly reported, but HHS has not reviewed cost reports for this information since then. While a repeal of the safe harbor provision would require a clearer understanding of the impact of the GPO funding structure, hospitals' potential underreporting of administrative fee revenue presents an immediate risk that can be addressed within the current GPO funding structure.

Recommendation for Executive Action

To help ensure the accuracy of Medicare's payments to hospitals, we recommend that the Secretary of the Department of Health and Human Services determine whether hospitals are appropriately reporting administrative fee revenues on their Medicare cost reports and take steps to address any under-reporting that may be found.

Agency and Third-Party Comments and Our Evaluation

We provided a draft of this report to HHS, FTC, and DOJ for comment. In its written response, reproduced in appendix II, HHS agreed with our recommendation, and stated that it will add steps to its process for auditing hospitals' cost reports so that contractors may review administrative fee revenues that hospitals receive from GPOs. We received technical comments from HHS, FTC, and DOJ which we incorporated as appropriate.

We also received comments on a draft of this report from the 5 GPOs in our review and from HSCA. Many of the comments we received were similar and include the following:

- Some of the GPOs and HSCA noted that they were concerned that the draft title was not consistent with the content of the report. We reconsidered this title in light of their concerns and believe the revised title—Group Purchasing Organizations: Funding Structure Has Potential Implications for Medicare Costs—addresses their concerns, but is still consistent with the findings of the report.

- Some of the GPOs and HSCA disagreed with the draft report's characterization that repeal of the safe harbor would have potential short-term disruption on the supply chain, stating that there would be significant market disruption that could result in higher healthcare costs. The draft report included statements we obtained from the GPOs—as well as experts and others—on the potential impact of eliminating the safe harbor. However, the draft report did not include a recommendation to repeal the safe harbor, noting that there is limited empirical evidence to definitively assess the impact of the vendor fee-based funding structure protected under the safe harbor.

- Some of the GPOs commented that the example about a subsidiary of a GPO with an alternative funding structure does not indicate that a model like this could support the entire industry if the safe harbor were repealed. The draft report only describes this as one possible example, and we added additional context to the report to clarify this point.

- Some of the GPOs and HSCA noted that there is currently no evidence that hospitals are not appropriately accounting for revenue received from GPOs on their cost reports and that GAO did not consider the findings of the 2005 HHS-OIG audit reports. However, we did consider the 2005 audit findings, and we added additional detail on them to the report. As noted in the draft report, the HHS-OIG recommended in 2005 that CMS provide specific guidance on the proper treatment of revenue distributions and, in 2011, CMS issued updated guidance on this issue. Since that updated guidance, HHS has not assessed whether revenues from GPOs are being appropriately accounted for.

- Some of the GPOs and HSCA noted that our draft report did not explain the reasons for the 20 percent increase in GPO administrative fees between 2008 and 2012. We added a statement to the report to describe the reasons why the total volume of fees may have increased, such as increased customer purchasing volume. In addition, the draft report examined changes in the percentage of fees collected, noting that these were generally consistent over this 4-year period.

- Some of the GPOs and HSCA stated that the draft report did not explain the full set of benefits of the GPO industry. We added some additional information to the report to more fully describe the activities and reported benefits of GPOs and how they serve hospitals or other providers. However, the scope of this report is focused on GPO contracting practices and funding structure. In a prior report, we described the services offered by GPOs and that work is referenced in this report. (See GAO-10-738).

- Some of the GPOs and HSCA commented that in describing the literature on the GPO funding structure, we do not include a discussion of any of the independent and industry funded studies on the impact of GPOs. As we state in the report, while we identified other studies that presented empirical data focused more broadly on the value of GPOs, these studies did not include evidence that directly addressed the effects of the GPO funding structure. In addition, some GPOs and HSCA noted that the study described in our report was funded by the Medical Device Manufacturers Association (MDMA). We added a note to the report that explains that MDMA provided funding for the author to purchase the data used in this study.

- Some of the GPOs raised concerns about the sample size and selection of vendors and hospitals we interviewed and stated that a broader sample of vendors and hospitals is necessary to maintain a more meaningful representation of their points of view. The information we obtained from hospitals and vendors was used to provide context and examples. We added a statement to the report to note that this information was not generalizable.

- Some of the GPOs commented that the description of FTC complaints is incomplete. We report FTC's comments on this matter and this report has been reviewed by FTC.

- Some GPOs commented that the draft report did not include a description of the GPO governance process or advisory board decision making. We added this information to the report.

We also received technical comments from the GPOs and HSCA which we incorporated as appropriate.

As agreed with your offices, unless you announce the contents of this report earlier, we plan no further distribution of it until 30 days from the report date. At that time, we will send copies of this report to the Secretary of the Department of Health and Human Services, the Attorney General, the Chairman of the Federal Trade Commission, and appropriate congressional committees. The report will be available at no charge on the GAO website at http://www.gao.gov.

If you or your staff have any questions concerning this report, please contact Linda T. Kohn at (202) 512-7114 or KohnL@gao.gov. Contact points for our Offices of Congressional Relations and Public Affairs may be found on the last page of this report. Other major contributors to this report are listed in appendix III.

Linda T. Kohn
Director, Health Care

List of Requesters

The Honorable Henry A. Waxman
Ranking Member
Committee on Energy and Commerce
House of Representatives

The Honorable Anna G. Eshoo
Ranking Member
Subcommittee on Communications and Technology
Committee on Energy and Commerce
House of Representatives

The Honorable Frank Pallone, Jr.
Ranking Member
Subcommittee on Health
Committee on Energy and Commerce
House of Representatives

The Honorable Diana DeGette
Ranking Member
Subcommittee on Oversight and Investigations
Committee on Energy and Commerce
House of Representatives

The Honorable Edward J. Markey
United States Senate

The Honorable John D. Dingell
House of Representatives

Appendix I: Scope and Methodology

Our objectives were to describe (1) Group Purchasing Organization (GPO) contracting practices and the reported effects of these practices; (2) how GPOs are funded and the reported effects of this funding structure.

To address these objectives, we sent a questionnaire to the five largest national GPOs by purchasing volume: Amerinet, HealthTrust Purchasing Group, MedAssets, Novation, and Premier. We asked about their contracting practices and sources of revenue, including administrative fees collected from vendors. We fielded the questionnaire from December 2013 through March 2014. One GPO did not provide answers through our web-based questionnaire. Rather, the GPO provided a separate document with answers to some of the questions, and sometimes in a different format than was requested. We clarified this GPO's responses through follow-up questions. Through our questionnaire, we asked about each GPO's

- purchasing volume by fiscal year, from 2000-2012;[1]
- purchasing volume by category of medical product for fiscal years 2000, 2004, 2008, and 2012;
- average, highest, lowest, and most frequent administrative fee percentages received in fiscal year 2012, by category of medical product;
- total dollar amount of administrative fees received in fiscal years 2000, 2004, 2008, 2012, by category of medical product;
- average, highest, lowest, and most frequent licensing fee percentages received in fiscal year 2012, by category of medical product;
- total dollar amount of licensing fees received in fiscal years 2000, 2004, 2008, 2012, by category of medical product;
- average, highest, lowest, and most frequent fee percentages for any fee that was based on a percentage of the purchasing price of a product in fiscal year 2012, by category of medical product;
- total dollar amount of total fees based on a percentage of the purchasing price of a product received in fiscal years 2000, 2004, 2008, and 2012, by category of medical product;

---

[1]GPOs fiscal years varied.

- total dollar amount of total fees based on the purchasing price of a product received in fiscal years 2000-2012;

- average, highest, lowest, and most frequent administrative fee percentages received in fiscal year 2012 for generic injectable drugs;

- average, highest, lowest, and most frequent licensing fee percentages received in fiscal year 2012 for generic injectable drugs;

- total dollar amount and percentage of administrative fees shared with customers and owners in fiscal year 2012;

- sources of revenue in fiscal year 2012;

- services provided to customers in fiscal year 2012 and how those services were funded;

- whether the GPO awarded, or had in effect, any sole-source, bundled, non-bid, or long-term contracts with vendors; and

- key ways that GPOs bring value to their customers.

We reported only the information that was consistently reported by most of the GPOs in our review. There were several questions that some GPOs did not answer, or did not answer completely, including, for example, the following:

- For questions requesting information over time, only two of the GPOs reported information for the entire time period. One GPO was able to report information back to fiscal year 2003, and two other GPOs were only able to report information back to fiscal year 2008. Representatives from both of these GPOs stated that their records retention policies prevented them from obtaining data before fiscal year 2008.

- For questions requesting information to be broken into multiple product categories, one GPO was unable to separately report information for medical devices and commodities. As a result, this GPO reported information for both categories combined. Another GPO reported that, for the purposes of the questionnaire, the GPO only considered cardiac and orthopedic products to be "devices." Other products considered to be devices by the Food and Drug Administration (FDA) were included in either the commodities or "other" categories.

In addition, we interviewed representatives with knowledge of GPOs, including

- the five largest GPOs to clarify their questionnaire responses, and discuss their contracting practices, funding structure, and the GPO safe harbor provision in more depth.

- two regional GPOs about how they work with the larger, national GPOs: Greater New York Hospital Association Services, Inc., and APS Healthcare.

- purchasing departments of five hospitals and hospital systems about how the hospitals purchase medical products, the extent of the hospitals' use of GPOs, additional services and total value they receive from their GPOs, and potential impacts on hospitals if the GPO safe harbor provision were repealed: the Dana Farber Cancer Institute, Mt. Sinai Medical Center, the University of Pittsburgh Medical Center, BJC Healthcare, and Intermountain Healthcare. We selected hospitals based on variation in: number of hospital beds, the extent to which the hospital had an ownership interest in a GPO, and which GPOs they used.

- eight vendors of medical products about GPO contracting practices, funding structure, and the GPO safe harbor provision: 3M; ICU Medical; Alcon; Teva Pharmaceutical Industries, Ltd.; Hospira; Fresenius Kabi USA; GlaxoSmithKline; AADCO Medical, Inc. We selected vendors based on variation in the types of products manufactured.

- trade associations representing GPOs and vendors of medical products about their members' relationships with GPOs, GPO contracting practices and funding structure, and the GPO safe harbor provision: Healthcare Supply Chain Association, Health Industry Distributors Association, Advanced Medical Technology Association, Medical Device Manufacturers Association, Generic Pharmaceutical Association.

In addition, to determine the reported effects of the GPO funding structure, we interviewed thirteen experts in economics, the healthcare market, and purchasing cooperatives. We identified these experts through our search of the relevant literature on GPOs, healthcare markets, purchasing cooperatives, and economics: David Balto, Roger Blair, Lawton Burns, Einer Elhauge, Adam Fein, Herbert Hovenkamp, Michael Lindsay, Diana Moss, Eugene Schneller, LeRoy Schwartz, Prakash Sethi, Hal Singer, Dave Swanson.

Finally, we interviewed Federal Trade Commission (FTC), Department of Justice (DOJ) and Health and Human Services (HHS) officials about their oversight of GPOs, including complaints they had received about GPOs and any investigations they had opened or actions they had taken against GPOs since our 2012 report.

To identify literature on the effect of the GPO funding structure, we conducted a literature review. To conduct this review, we searched 28 bibliographic databases, such as ProQuest and MEDLINE, for articles published between January 2004 and June 2014. In our search, we used a combination of search terms such as "group purchasing" and "health care."[2] We considered an article relevant to our review if it discussed the potential effects of the GPO funding structure. Using the articles we identified as relevant to our review, we then determined which of these articles included the results of empirical analyses. To confirm that our search captured all of the relevant literature that met our criteria, we reviewed the bibliographies of the relevant articles to identify other potentially relevant studies. We did not assess the methodologies of the studies we identified or review the reliability of the data used in these studies.

In addition, we reviewed documentary evidence of the factors that GPOs consider when contracting for products and services, including scorecards, spreadsheets, and other templates provided by the GPOs. We reviewed published articles in economic and law journals, as well as analyses of the healthcare market. We also reviewed laws, legislative history, regulations and guidance related to the GPO safe harbor.

---

[2]Our search terms included the following: "group purchasing," "purchasing alliance," "pooling alliance," "hospital," "physician," "healthcare," "health care," "provider," and "nursing home."

Appendix II: Comments from the Department of Health and Human Services

DEPARTMENT OF HEALTH & HUMAN SERVICES   OFFICE OF THE SECRETARY

Assistant Secretary for Legislation
Washington, DC 20201

OCT 3 2014

Linda T. Kohn
Director, Health Care
U.S. Government Accountability Office
441 G Street NW
Washington, DC 20548

Dear Ms. Kohn

Attached are comments on the U.S. Government Accountability Office's (GAO) report entitled,
"Group Purchasing Organizations: Funding Structure has Potential to Inflate Medicare Costs"
(GAO-15-13).

The Department appreciates the opportunity to review this report prior to publication.

Sincerely,

Jim R. Esquea
Assistant Secretary for Legislation

Attachment

**GENERAL COMMENTS OF THE DEPARTMENT OF HEALTH AND HUMAN
SERVICES (HHS) ON THE GOVERNMENT ACCOUNTABILITY OFFICE'S REPORT
ENTITLED: GROUP PURCHASING ORGANIZATIONS: FUNDING STRUCTURE
HAS POTENTIAL TO INFLATE MEDICARE COSTS (GAO-15-13)**

The Department of Health and Human Services (HHS) appreciates the opportunity to review and
comment on this draft report.

GAO Recommendation

To help ensure the accuracy of Medicare's payments to hospitals, we recommend that the
Secretary of the Department of Health and Human Services determine whether hospitals are
appropriately reporting administrative fee revenues on their Medicare cost reports and take steps
to address any under-reporting that may be found.

HHS Response

HHS concurs with this recommendation. HHS will add steps to the audit process so that
contractors may review Group Purchasing Organization (GPO) administrative fee revenues.
There are currently audit steps for contractors to identify rebates, allowances and refunds of
expenses (per 42 CFR 413.98), but additional steps will be included specifically for GPOs. It
should be noted that expenses are not reviewed on a routine basis for all providers. If expenses
are reviewed during the audit process, the contractor will attempt to ensure GPO expenses, if
they exist, are reported properly.

HHS thanks GAO for their efforts on this issue and looks forward to working with GAO on this
and other issues in the future.

Appendix III: GAO Contact and Staff Acknowledgments

GAO Contacts	Linda T. Kohn, (202) 512-7114 or kohnl@gao.gov
Acknowledgments	In addition to the contact named above, Kristi Peterson, Assistant Director; Kelly DeMots; Leia Dickerson; Sandra George; and Yesook Merrill made key contributions to this report.